God's Great Plan

An overview of the Bible for Kids

By Diana Moss

Published by New Generation Publishing in 2021

First Edition

ISBN: 978-1-80369-100-8

www.newgeneration-publishing.com

New Generation Publishing

God's love story to the world

for Hope

Thank you Jim for your proofreading

In the beginning, before the earth and heavens were made there was only God. Nothing had any form. There was no day or night. There was no sun or moon, no stars in the sky. There were no fish or animals. There were no flowers or birds. There weren't any people. Everything was darkness. Everything was still and silent.

And then the Lord God said, "Let there be light" and there was light. God separated the light from the darkness to make day and night. He separated the waters so there were seas and an atmosphere around the earth. He spoke again and the waters rolled back so that dry land appeared and mountains rose. God made the sun and the moon and the stars so we would have seasons and signs in the heavens.

God spoke again and there were fruit trees and flowers of all kinds.

He spoke and the oceans filled with living creatures from the smallest plankton to the great sea monsters that live in some parts of the ocean. At God's command beasts appeared upon the earth – tigers, lions, bears, rabbits and mice, elephants, lizards, frogs, bees and ants, and many more.

Everything was good and perfect and beautiful.

When it was all ready, when plants were making air to breathe, when animals, birds and fish were making sounds and movement, the Lord God bent down and took some dust from the earth and from this He formed a man. He made the man in the image of Himself, and then He breathed the breath of life into the man's nostrils. He took this man and placed him in a garden He had prepared. God brought all the creatures He had made before the man and let him name them. They belonged to the man in the same way that you belong to your father and mother who named you. But there wasn't a creature anywhere suitable to be a helper to the man, so the Lord made him fall asleep. He took a rib from the man's side and made a woman for him. She was bone of his bone and flesh of his flesh, and they were perfect for one another.

The man's name was Adam and his wife's name was Eve. They lived together with God in the Garden of Eden. God liked all He had made in just six days. He rested on the seventh day. Life was perfect.

God also made other creatures called angels and seraphim and cherubim. These creatures were to serve the Lord God, to worship and praise Him, and to minister to all the men and women who would come from Adam and Eve. One was very beautiful. His name was Lucifer and he became so proud of his beauty that he thought he was as good as God. Not only that but he thought he should have the same power as God. So he fought a war in heaven and God threw him out, along with those angels who had sided with Lucifer. One third of the angels in heaven fell to earth. They are still here. And they are still fighting against God. Lucifer goes by other names, terrible names, names you know and fear; Satan, Beelzebub, Serpent of old. His helpers are called demons, but we are all safe because God loves and protects us.

Then Satan, appearing as a serpent, slithered into the Garden that God had made for Adam and Eve.

The serpent spoke to Eve saying, "Has God said you should eat of any tree in the garden?"

Actually God had said they could eat from any tree in the garden except one that was the tree of knowledge of good and evil.

Eve got muddled by Satan's question and said that God had told them they could eat from any of the trees except one, the tree of knowledge of good and evil. If they even were to touch it they would die. The evil one said, "Surely you won't die!"

Satan lied to Eve and told her that if she ate from the tree she would be just like God.

Eve thought that sounded wonderful so she went and looked at the forbidden tree. It was very beautiful, as everything was in God's garden, and she wanted what Satan said she could have. So she took the fruit, bit into it and ate it.

Then she gave the fruit to Adam her husband and he ate some as well. He should have known better, but he did it anyway. With that single act of disobedience, sin entered the world and brought death with it.

This made God very sad and angry, but He still loved Adam and Eve. He made clothing from animal skin for Adam and Eve. (This sacrifice points forward to Jesus's sacrifice for us on the cross many years later.) Then He made Adam and Eve leave the Garden. Ever since that time people have had to work very hard to make a living. We have pain and sorrow. We're afraid. We hurt one another in all kinds of horrid ways. We're all just like Adam and Eve. We have a sinful nature now. Even when we know what's right, sometimes we do wrong. And it only takes a little sin (or doing something wrong) to make a person a sinner. Adam and Eve couldn't be close to God any more. They didn't have a strong friendship with Him like they'd had before in the Garden when He walked and talked with them face to face.

God loved them still and He loves us too. He's our Father and He wants us back again very much. Right from the beginning, God knew we would make bad choices. So He had already made a plan to give us a way back to Him. God would one day send a Messiah; someone Who would rescue everyone from all the wrong things they had done.

Now Adam and Eve had three sons, Cain, Abel and Seth. Cain was so jealous of Abel that he killed him. These events happened thousand of years ago but they still apply to us today. From that time evil spread all over the world. Then Seth's family stopped worshipping God as dependent creatures and became like Cain's cocky family.

A few years later there was Noah. Noah was a good man and walked faithfully before God.

God said to him, "I am going to put an end to all people, because the earth is filled with violence because of them. I want you to make a big boat which will be called an ark."

This seemed a crazy thing to tell him to do, but Noah believed God and obeyed. When Noah had built his massive boat, he loaded it up with two of every living animal on earth, just as God had told him to.

Then down came the rain. It rained so much that the whole earth was flooded.

God saved Noah's whole family by making sure that the ark floated. God then made a rainbow in the sky as His promise that He would never again flood the earth like He did then.

This shows us that God takes it very seriously when we sin by trying rule our own lives, but it assures us that God has made a way for all of us to be forgiven. Much later on God's Son even became a carpenter like Noah so that whoever trusts in Jesus can be saved.

Some years after that there was a man called Abraham. Abraham was a complete nobody, worshipping creatures instead of his Creator God. Yet when God called him, Abraham gave up everything to become a nomad, living in a tent. He married Sarah and they had a son when he was very old. Abraham's son Isaac was a nobody too, yet his son Jacob believed God and risked everything to follow Him. Jacob's eleventh-born son Joseph was a nobody too. He used to boast about things. In fact he annoyed his brothers so much that they pretended to their father that Joseph was dead. What those brothers had actually done was to sell Joseph to some slave traders who were going to Egypt. Life for Joseph was very hard, but because Joseph trusted God in difficult times, he eventually became the Egyptian prime minister and was able to save both his family and the most powerful nation in the world from starvation.

God's people became known as the Hebrews. The Egyptian pharaoh was cruel and made slaves of them. God raised up Moses, another nobody to plan the greatest escape story in world history. Moses asked Pharaoh to let the Hebrew slaves go. Pharaoh said no.

Egypt then suffered lots of plagues. The Hebrew slaves eventually escaped from Egypt, but they were followed by the Egyptian army. Just as they seemed to catch up with the Hebrews, God made a path through the Red Sea so that they walked through it on dry land. As the Egyptians followed, the sea came back and drowned them.

The Hebrews wandered in the desert for forty long years while God provided them with miraculous food and drink. Then came the time to go into the Promised Land that God had for them. The Promised Land was called Israel and is still called that today. The Hebrew people who lived there became known as Israelites.

God gave Moses the ten commandments to take to the people. These laws were good and perfect and given by God but it was a terrible burden. People needed the laws to help them obey God again, but the law also taught the men, women and children that they couldn't seem to obey every one of them. There were so many laws about so many things, nobody, not one single person could keep them all. Some didn't care, but others wanted to please God. The problem was, if you broke one law, that made you a lawbreaker and a sinner. (That is someone who does wrong things.) And the punishment for sin is death.

God told the Israelites that He would accept a perfect sheep or goat so that people didn't have to die. That person must buy the animal and take it to the high priest. Then the high priest would accept it on God's behalf as a sacrifice for what the person had done wrong.

Then the Israelites decided they wanted a proper king like other countries had. Up until then God had ruled over them. King Saul was their first king, but he got too proud about being king and often did bad things. God then appointed a lowly shepherd called David to be the next king of Israel. Before he actually became king, David was very brave and killed a giant called Goliath. David wrote lots of songs which are called psalms in our bible. He was a good king.

David had a son called Solomon. He wrote some songs too. When David died Solomon became king and he was known for being very wise. As the years went by there were other kings too.

God then told several people called prophets that He would send a Messiah who would save the world. He would come to rescue and save people from all the wrong things they had done. The people often cried out "When will the Messiah come to rescue us?"

Hundreds of years passed by and there were terrible wars and famines and droughts. Death and Satan never take a holiday. The people would follow the laws and try to be good, and then they would forget again and be very very bad.

God would send men called prophets to call the people back to Him. "I am your Father. I love you. Come to Me. Come to Me."

Sometimes the people listened, and were sorry for what they had done. When they didn't their enemies would come and capture them, drag them away from their homes and make them slaves. Then the people would cry out again. "Oh Lord, when will the Messiah come to rescue us?"

Hundreds of years passed by.

When God knew it was exactly the right time He sent an angel called Gabriel to a young girl named Mary and told her that she was going to have a baby. Not only that, but this baby was going to be God's only Son, Jesus, the Messiah who would come to rescue the people. Mary didn't understand as she wasn't even married, but the angel told Mary that God's Holy Spirit was going to overshadow her and she would become pregnant. So that's what happened. God saw to everything, even to providing Mary with a godly husband called Joseph who was a carpenter.

At that time everyone had to return to their birthplace in order to be counted. Joseph and Mary travelled to Bethlehem. Mary was almost ready to give birth to Jesus. They couldn't find anywhere to stay. Finally they found shelter in a stable. When Jesus was born Mary and Joseph were so poor all they could do was wrap the baby in cloths and lay Him in an animal's feeding trough, keeping Him warm with some hay.

Then an amazing thing happened just as Jesus was born. Some angels appeared in the sky praising God and some nearby shepherds were quite frightened. The angels told them about Jesus so they went to see Him and worshipped Him. A new star shone in the sky. It was a sign from God that He had sent the Messiah at last!

Sadly not many people noticed it, but three men who studied the stars noticed it and they even followed that star as it led them out of their own country. Then it stopped right over the place where Jesus had been born. They knew it meant that someone important had been born and they wanted to go and worship Him. They didn't know Jesus was the King of kings and *the* God, the only God, the One who had created everything that ever was or would be.

The men made the mistake of making enquiries at the palace before they found Jesus. King Herod was very jealous and asked the men to tell him where the new King was so that he could worship him too. In fact Herod had already decided that when he found him, he was going to kill this little baby.

Happily, after finding Jesus and giving Him gifts, the men returned home another way. Then God told Joseph in a dream to take Mary and Jesus away to live in Egypt for a while.

Jesus grew up and became a carpenter like Joseph. He chose twelve men to be his disciples, (special friends) and He did many miracles, making sick people better because He loved them so much. He talked to them a lot about God's love.

The Jewish leaders liked to think that they obeyed the law in every detail, so when they spotted Jesus doing something they thought He shouldn't do, they didn't like it one bit. Even though Jesus only ever did good things out of love, the Jewish leaders hated Him. They were angry because they'd expected Jesus to be a warrior Messiah and lead them into battle against the hated Romans. The Romans wanted peace at any price even if it meant killing an innocent man.

So, although Jesus had done nothing wrong, they killed Him!

Everyone took part. Even you and me, despite us not actually being there at the time. We do wrong things just like they did.

Sadly they had Jesus put to death. He hadn't done anything wicked, but He suffered a very cruel death, as He was nailed to a wooden cross outside Jerusalem and hung from His hands and feet until He died. Satan must have thought he had won the battle as Jesus died that day.

How he must have celebrated when they took Jesus' body down to be buried.

Jesus was only a young man aged thirty-three and He didn't even have a burial place prepared for Him. They had to lay the only Son of God in a borrowed tomb which was closed by rolling a very heavy stone in front of it. Soldiers were told to guard it.

Those who had loved Jesus lost all hope. They hid themselves away and wept.

Three days later some women went to anoint Jesus' body with herbs and spices but when they got to the tomb, the big stone had been rolled away!

It was open! There was nobody there! The women were even more sad and began to cry. It was then that Jesus appeared to them because He had been raised back to life!

Jesus lived on this earth, appearing to His friends and many more people. Then after a few weeks His disciples watched Jesus as He rose up into heaven. Jesus had told them that He would send His Holy Spirit to live among them. This He did, and this is how He lives in and among us today.

Jesus is still alive to this very day! Anyone who believes in Jesus will never perish, but will have everlasting life and live with Him. Those who believe will shed their earthly bodies when they die and join Him in paradise. Death could not keep Him in the grave. Satan could not destroy Him. Jesus rose from the dead!

The human race will never be the same again. We don't like to admit that we need forgiveness. As humans we are always making excuses for ourselves. But the Bible's message talks about people feeling guilty, our fear of punishment and the sense that God is very far away. Jesus died and rose again to take away our guilt and to bring us back to God.

God knows all of our thoughts, so the gap between us is not just one of feeling guilty but also of feeling shame. Jesus dealt with this when He was stripped naked and hung on a cross for all the world to see. The people laughed at Him, spat at Him, not understanding who He really was.

What is your response to Jesus' death and resurrection?

He offers you three things; forgiveness, freedom and hope for the future.

But He also asks you to *admit* that you are a sinful nobody who needs a Saviour. He asks you to *believe* His death and resurrection have given you all the salvation you need. He asks you to *commit* your life to Him, giving all you have to the One who transformed history through His bloodied cross and empty tomb.

In return you will know that you are so special and precious to Him and that you are loved like you have never been loved before. He will guide you every day if you ask Him to.

I have made my decision.

Have you made yours?

Think about it.

Now tell God that you want to become part of His salvation story.

Lightning Source UK Ltd.
Milton Keynes UK
UKHW021551111221
395420UK00006B/149